Mid-Season Flowers

Mid-Season Flowers

by

Daniel Robert Lewis

2024

This book is dedicated to the Muse of Poetry, whose lively spirit has called upon me throughout my years to, if nothing else, enchant me with these words, as they were not intended for anyone else to gaze upon.

Contents

Preface

    This collection of poems, dating from 2008 to 2015, forms the uncollected poetry from my twenties, being eighty-one poems in all. They don't exactly belong to any other collection, and so I put them here together, whether they seem to work or not. I say "work" since they're rather different (or feel different to me, at the least, probably due to the expanse of time since having written them, since, when I look back at my many poems, my style and interests have changed a little, yet they still remain similar over the years), but then I've written so much that sometimes what I write is bound to be a little bit different from any sort of ordinary way I write, whatever that happens to be. I view some of these poems as experimental as a result of that, and, as such, some of them—to me at least—come across as more interesting than do others.

    My previous collection like this, *Flowers from my Youth*, collected the bulk of poetry I wrote in my teens, in that case, from 2002-2005, 2002 being the start of my poetical writings (and there's still a bunch of hard-to-decipher poems left from late 2003 to mid-2004 that could form another collection alone, that's how prolific I was); and so I see myself over these years as having grown and matured not only as a writer, but as a poet. I still find my old works interesting over all these years that pass by, for I covered a lot of territory concerning whatever it was I happened to be writing and thinking about. My poetical works, like most poet's, to some degree relate to my own life, and so are not entirely made up—though much of mine is, but anytime we write, there is a part of ourselves that goes in to it too, making it semi-autobiographical, whether we meant it to be or not, we are present there.

As it happens, only in the mid-2000s did I begin to really "look" at my writings and revise them at all, and so when I started writing poems again in my twenties (I have no poems at all, apparently, from 2006-2007, which is unfortunate, unless something has been misplaced, which is always possible) I viewed them with a more critical eye than before. Needless to say these poems seemed, at the time of writing, better than how I wrote during my teens, as even when I was in my early twenties I couldn't help but notice some improvements in my writing, just from having lived life and gained new experiences, if nothing else; and so I hope that comes across as true with the reader as well. All of these poems were revised, of course, as too many of them weren't properly gone over in the first place, and some not read at all in a number of years; some even lacked consistency in spots, having written them hastily, but with just a few scant revisions at the time—all part of the writer's life. However, their fundamental structures remain, and at that, the bulk of them remain unchanged as well, as I tend to go a little more lightly on these older poems than I would present-day ones, that's just how it goes with me.

The first poem is almost a breath of fresh air, since it was the first in three years and some months since having written a poem. Those first four were written on regular 8.5x11 paper, and then after that I took them out of two journals that had collected them. A few of the others were also on regular paper: "In My Time," "Not My Day," and "Temple," all of which were on the same paper. The date of May 17, 2009, was clearly special, having written twelve poems on the same day, and that marked a sort of Renaissance that brought me back into the habit of regular poetry writing, though not quite as much as 2003-2004 was, but still, it felt like a lost love remembered and cherished once again.

There are some poems in here that seem to be very personal and about my own life experiences, such as "Seeing You" and "Feelings for You," but they are wholly made up, rest assured. I'm a writer who utilizes the imagination to a great degree, whether or not I've ever experienced something (to any of my readers of *Wandering Flowers*, they'll remember that some of the later poems are set in actual Hell). Regardless, there are times I've taken real-life experiences and used them in my writings, but very often they are mere descriptions added in here and there, and not the entirety of the writing, and so even here I'm unable to point out a single poem that was wholly inspired by an actual event or experience. Many other modern-day poets often write about themselves, but that's never been me!

At the end of the collection there is only one poem for 2014 and one for 2015, and that is because *Wandering Flowers* took up the bulk of those years, including some from earlier years as well. Along with that I did six short poetry collections under an alias from 2014-2015 that naturally won't be seen here, and so I still did get around to writing a bit of poetry at that time.

I hope that the reader of *Mid-Season Flowers* will enjoy them for what they are: attempts at beautifying the world a little more; but also, if there is any chance for inspiration for their own poetical writings or musings about life, perhaps it will do something other than just be "reading more boring old poems" again, for I do believe that poetry can change our lives for the good if we can only find the path towards such a life, something this world is desperately short of (let alone people who read at all). And with that I hope that you, the reader, get lost in a world of fanciful images, the like of which are not often enough seen.

Mid-Season Flowers

Shadows   12/12/08

Shadows—
my darkest desire.
They have no color
but darkness.

Over land
(bleakly met),
standing forever:
a tree.

Sailing there
on a ship.
A sudden death—
the plague.

No more rays.
Losing all hope;
speaking so truly
of freedom's end.

Time devours heavenly bodies
throughout this; our lives
are left with nothing but
shadows.

The fungi have arrived
here in the well,
growing so strong,
plump, and swell.

When dawn comes
the fungi will dance,
up the walls,
up the street,
all in a row,
two-toed and fleet.

Forever is today and
never is ever;
light trickles down earth,
as it enters tomorrow
to the world where
the fungi will be.

Lives are not the same:
they live, play, and dance
all for one day,
but by dusk,
they are free.

Pimpernels   12/18/08

Out there,
five bright petals strong:
where shall these little guys thrive
in the great big world?
High up in life's sky
they will see a light
to make them grow
and reveal themselves
as the prettified spectacles
that they are.

The one that,
at your end,
spits on your name,
even as you paid in gold
to embellish your shallow soul.
You saved lives despite
your inner nature;
sacrificed everything in the name
of goodness;
accepted no gratitude,
no bidding to this great cause;
righteousness was your twin,
and yet still
Diabolos can see
a crack,
a blemish—nay,
a flaw.
In this mere human soul,
it speaks indefinable language,
unforgiving and not caring for others,
a melancholic soul
now standing on trial,
the trial for your eternity,
all towards striving to find
a just end
to your ultimate destination.
This once courageous,
once kind and generous
peace-loving soul is who

is on trial.
And dare the accuser accuse
this good person
of something so trivial-seeming
as the annihilation of a
colony of ants that lived
in his basement?
Some *force* possessed him
in that moment, it overcame
him, telling him to destroy them all.
Poisoned, they died slowly and painfully.
Guilty of committing mass murder,
this man thoroughly fumigated the
scene of his crimes and, indeed,
his whole house,
and so it was nonviable
for the ants to ever find a
shelter there, for and from
whatever reason.
This is the damnable evidence
against this once-thought-to-be-
oh-so-good soul.

Will he or won't he?
That is the question,
but what will the answer be?

Ice

Cracking, ripping,
breaking apart,
all during a day of crimson weather.
You find not one
but thousands of little
shards of ice,
resembling melting glass,
drifting under an eternal sky,
waiting for the day to end.

Lamp   5/17/09

It rests there like a king,
its grace not flaunting the
slightest speck of dust.
It's never alone,
but surrounded by
lavishly decorated ornaments.
It rules the night,
knowing it can wield
no candle towards its
arch-rival, the sun.
But both remain content
in their relative positions.

In the stillness,
yet present.
Soft, yet hard.
Both fantastically
black and white,
and yet succeeding
in being neither =
both states at once.

Yes: questions mark the answers,
and rhymes never meet
their appropriate ends.

Falling trees still sound
while being in a lone field.

Today, being a new day,
you are in truth
quite alive, a riddle
bespeaking your very
own nature; but also
quintessentially nothing,
and in between it all
fancy-free, delighting
in the caretaking of little things,
until life finds another
purpose for you,
a road taken differently,
one never before experienced,
whispering through the

breath of time,
reasons to remain here.

And so we move to
another song being played
as the world shifts beneath
our feet.

The Chair

The day was hard,
the felling of trees
evidenced on my person,
and so what could be
more fitting than to sit on
a throne of wood in repose—
a great way
to end the day.

Fantasy   5/17/09

So little distance the world goes from here,
tickling the fancied feet
until you cry,
wearing green shirts that carry
red buttons and blue trim.
They spray their lucid thoughts
so joyfully,
bewildering those unexpected visitors
with wonder and astonishment.

The trees have gone.
A feral scent pervades the
forest path—hinting at what?
Of a robust nature, and youthful,
maybe,
but the fresh song permeated the
old path, one that never goes away.
I feel an awe
at something benign
but lovely, vanishing traces
of which catch
the faintest glimpse of
an eternal summoning presence
felt through the trees,
for there is a spirit
in the woods.

Birds don't despair in gloom,
for they fly through the carnival of life,
with plenty of room for
dreams.

Birds don't smile,
yet they fly in freedom
above the lands they seek,
never burdening themselves
with illusions of grandeur,
not wanting, nor influenced to be
anything but their bare,
natural self.

And so to the birds I
see above me,
I say,
"Go fly away."

Idle   5/17/09

Masters from beyond, pouring
into my life their words
of forbidden lore and
arcane wisdom,
ever so tiresome upon my soul
that is waning today,
for it won't awaken
again without a "good morning."

Thoughts on a thinking day,
molesting my happy mind of
any sanity contained herein,
and nothing more remained
save for the little buttercups
growing outside my porch.

Markets are not a slave trade,
nor a stale bread stand
lost to its owner—
its owner recently made
a trip to the Moon—
and so it is known that
ants do not tarry,
nor do mockingbirds go astray;
there's no place here for
a goblin market,
nor the advertisement for
a non-workable teleportation device
via tachyon particles;
but you may find comfort yet,
pilgrim, in knowing that
your journey of consequence
was not conducted in vain;
nor was it vain to witness
Gregorian chanting,
or to see the end of the year
of 2002, December 31st;
and so let there be light on your
journey to yonder marketplace.

Nodding off in the light
daze of the midday sky,
already full bloom and half
upon the opening-up world,
we share our idle thoughts
like two sharecroppers arguing,
only we are worthless vagabonds,
travelers without words to
speak for ourselves, muttering
nonsense in non-rhythmical utterances,
spewing out vulgar phrases not
for us, but to the painful
ground we tread,
viewing various
aspects of life with no serious
tone of voice, imagining advice
that is hanging from paper planes
only to be found in the
exotic lands
of Spain;
seeing nauseous amounts of gloriously
bright days; watching flowers
dancing at break of day,
even ones that manage to grow
on a fungal floor;
being atoned at a grave,
the very same night of which
an answer came in the form
of a featureless face,

noticing the differences
between a prototype and a
dark power, sitting down
by a fire at an unusual hour;
dreaming dreams of time
and wondrously mind-bending
experimentations concerning
the true nature behind
space;
writing these drastic—nay—
contrived pieces of only
a part of poetry, taking into
consideration nothing but the
abstract art forms, I have,
for now, finished my
idling day.

May it be a day of the
future, or one of yesterday,
here I sit, writing what I will,
so much that cannot stop
me, my engines running at
maximum power.
You there, the finite reader,
shall be my guide.

Life in bloom,
vigorously flowing waves
heeding the beauty of early
salt air. Life is in.

Gone and forgotten,
the thoughts before sleep,
taking me where I don't
bother to know.

Life is May,
during which time it grows,
fluctuating upwards
towards no known end,
totally unaware of its
own destiny.

You could (you say)
climb up a tree . . .
run a barrel down a hill . . .
go mongoose hunting,
and still come out clean,
but in all this
you have used up
what made you *you*,
from before all this.

Melody   5/18/09

Lightly-hued colored petals
near an ethereal-like state,
dancing with the wind,
singing tunes written by the
melodies of the earth,
wishing away kisses under moonlight,
and having only one true thought:
being there.

Song   5/19/09

Songs of the earth,
little flowers,
sprinkled with morning dew,
kissing the fresh sunlight,
the air yielding to a
morning dove, on flight
across the verdant trees,
reaching across overseas,
seeking out foreign lands,
ones tuned in to nature
by music from an unknown hand;
and all of its wonderful children
are here to be found on this
glorious day.

Down the river's bend,
only dust withers.
Perfume all over
your beautiful body,
so ravishing a sight,
yet delicately frail,
but prettily framed
against the stained glass window
that guards the shower.

Wild geese roam
amongst children who are
ambushed by emotionally
inept parents,
discerning nothing
but flavors felt upon their
painted faces.

The rhythm of the earth
speaks:
a fertile season that
lives and graces
the clouds that are
not above us to shade
our evil thoughts,
but rather to bring despair over
the worriment of immature
but lovely persons who
will truly live forever
on this astral-like plane
of existing without knowing
it all, ever, in any final
respect, however blessed one is.
Let them cherish their time,
lasting but too briefly to
satisfy our hungry souls,
which are ready to get
up and shout "Vengeance!
Vengeance!" to all those
little people who dare
disagree with their noble
but personally biased opinions.
And so
rest in peace,
the living.

Darkly lit these bad feelings are,
destroying even angels
in their wake;
when amongst the pure
do we seek,
but with only feeble hope lying
before us.
It is there—
right over yonder—
there, where the songbirds
are,
in a pastoral land,
so far away,
speaking innocence
to us, its tongue stapled
shut from lifelong misery
of all the wrongs done
to its being,
playing endless lullabies
for all with a
discerning ear.

Innocent is a child's
breath
while sleeping so peacefully
on the forest floor,
more fit for a garden's dew,
the heartbeat of the flower bed
measured by each passing breath,
illuminating the senses to
the smell of a fresh rain pour—
a light rain—
seeping life into the old Earth,
emanating from the eternity
of Time,
while children sleep.

Withered,
the day gone by,
insight never lacking
on a rainy day,
so you speculate the times
away during a spike
of mass excellence,
a superb stature on just
one aspect of life;
and that is how to
end your day.

Will I cry myself to sleep,
or will I taste a wildflower on my tongue?
Perhaps I'll meet a friend
and light a bonfire with them
till the sun rises once again?
No, yet the day is here
for us to learn from,
watching the night phases
change their cloud dresses
for us, the people of the Earth.
Shall we rise to take this calling?
Seeding future images
offer enough thoughts
for roaming away in endless
plains of renewal.

Demeaning is you,
the false artist,
drawing pastiches in
satirizing format,
a self-effacing delusion
of an instance in
mockery.

Demeaning is you,
the absolute and total liar
of mankind,
who shall soon see
what is down on the
cusp of the Earth's
true core.

Demeaning is you,
a wicked, awful knave,
such a cruelly tortured
soul to have ever
existed, that the
marks made upon your
body do not suffice,
and this despite
the terrifying presence of
Azrael himself,
you do not have enough.

Demeaning is you
of the world,

of the void,
of the death
which becomes you.

Ever-present warmth,
touched by the sun,
as a baby cradled by love,
fresh speckles of green
with white signifying purity,
sparks a new relation;
the ongoing optimism
that is life, never to recede
into the shadows,
always conscious of the
magnificent world around it;
with such opalescent
beauty amplified,
the resounding effects
are one and all
for good, for justice,
ending never.

And then the strange . . .

In a dust-ridden corridor,
an effigy of yourself waits;
you cannot escape the dark;
there is no way out,
no way to go,
nowhere to run;
once subtle signs of happiness
have now become something
grotesque, a beast unseen,

the body of which a specter
could not shift;
a blackness encompassing
the land we choose to
live on,
that which is spoken,
only nightmarish incantations will
follow our unworthy tongues;
the inhumane deeds of which
we daily perform against and
not for our own kind is
unforgivable, and that
which we neglect to do
hurts others, if from nothing
but a memory lapse,
and we are fulfilled,
entrenched in destruction.

Only incense, air,
and toffee brew
work together, they said,
and kissed, they did,
golden tongues and all,
these solipsistic poets,
wandering aimlessly over
dark moors,
brooding thoughts worthy
of no one;
wasting what is precious;
defending not only life,
but honor as well;
your noble heart dead,
the stone wall
knows me very well,
being a gentle sort;
your soul glides, as is
the sun's way,
into a full-circled
oblivion;
and I,
a desperate, wretched creature,
cast out like a leper,
my own self abandoned,
worthless, and from no power
more powerful than my own words.

Paper is a way to
ramble, stumble, and fall—
to your knees, no less.
Certain of yourself,
you strive on for
good amongst the
ramblings people make,
wasting no time bickering
about a flaw in another's character;
and above all of this
is a thing known as life,
which happens to include
you too.

The coolness comes
through my soul,
aged or not;
I feel this
as vividly as when you
are sunned till the
skin burns, and not
able to peel it off
to cure, but rest away
for it to leave you.
And I say, the season
has now begun.

Eclipsed   11/16/10

Surrounded by feelings
that will betray;
enraptured in emotions
so brittle at bay;
opening new doorways
to a scene afar:
the future to be.

They come to warn you,
then to shun you;
you, the ostracized
one, a scapegoat to the people.

At large, yes, it seems
unfair to all who know,
all who shall live this
way.

Is it not enough?
You sacrificed for this
privilege, and now at a sum
so great, you succumb.

I imagined them as imps,
but their
atavistic ways belie
nothing more than that of
a beast untamed.
~ So says petty civilization.

You see her with him,
and him with her,
different groups, duos,
sets, or whatnots—and you,
alone in this particular
aspect.

The world does not
see an equal eye to
your liking, and so others,
though nice faces they
offer, have secondary
motives.

Growing up, alienation
is familiar to you,
and oh, dare you show
how you truly are to the
family, to be shut down
with desperate, sorry looks,
wishing you were that other
they had expectations for.

Damned from society (save
for your own kind),
spit on by your enemies,
a popular activity towards
your very type.

Can you say what you are?
Confession at the local pub will
bring no relief. Truth to
the self brings guilt
all about, shrouding
who you really are.

Then: justification, when
lying with friends.
Upon awakening: seeing them,
seeing you, happy as is,
wishing the best, for time
to stand still at this
very moment.

Knowledge in certainty of
who you are brings,
for now, confidence in
identifying self-traits.
As for vindication—a disease
to remain there in the head.

Hope . . . so many do. It is a good thing.
We do not give up.
We are survivors. So, as such,
you will go on as you are,
sickened by others as they
are of you, to live.

Stillness   11/17/10

It stands still,
balancing its footing,
supporting a solid frame—
one built to last.
Strength is its god,
as always, unchanged.
A stone heart,
an impossible body—
one with no flaws—
warmed only by the sun,
seen by the few,
who change as it knows no change.
And in it all,
a passive stare studies the
eternity ahead.

The worries, the pains—
will they go away?
Will this agony cease?
Never to let up,
going in, in to a
place against life,
yet to survive—
that is worth a million
tears of misery for
those who care to witness.

Do they love me?
Am I good-looking to their
subtle gaze?
The mirror has yet to show
age.
We made contact so
long ago now, it seems.
We felt one another's
lips, the essence of which
made a relationship bloom
into what could be a
lifestyle;
and after the magic
last night—
seeing you reveal
your inner self,
our talk of consequence
with each other,
dozing off in one another's arms—
and then, the next morning,
watching you get out of bed,
natural state observed,
wondering if it will always be
like this, a private little heaven,
soon to be forgotten.

If this could last forever,
and the love I truly felt
while with you, even if I

suffered some mental delusion
and it lasted a lifetime,
then it's the best dream a person
can have, that of
falling in love.

(Symmetries not working)
"My mind shut off
the production line,
memory a gray blank,
lined with wear,
pockmarked and rugged,
used over again repeatedly
as so many
unceasingly dull moments,
lacking in vivid imagination,"
I cannot but describe
this piece of artwork as.

Those who try
are doomed to fail,
for the sound of the scrying horn has been heard,
so that even if you are led the way,
you cannot but ultimately
be led astray.

Time =
the beginning.
We were this something
special they made,
all formed from absolute knowledge,
by one who ends the days.

Past Particle Phase   11/25/10

(Inspired by reading Joan of Arc's trial)

Impressions missing the
fleeting moments of when
past met present.

Did they torture that
way? Was it cold
the way you felt in
the cell?

The ghost of your
spirit—a sanctifying image—
has inspired, having
redeemed itself,
calling the Lord:
"O Lord, do not forsake me.
Time is not with me.
Death is seen like a
blanket before my face,
the embers burning.
Forgive me."

Cotton: Come and see O
Paper: Peoples of the world,
Leather: Later than not,
Wood: With hands clasped,
Wool: Wondrous joys seen upon
Tin: Timely saints as
Silk: St. Florian of Lorch is
Crystal: Calling from down below,
China: Calling from the water flow,
Silver: Since fish are so—
Pearl: Pearly-eyed mermaids
Ruby: Rummaging through his
Gold: Grave. Come and see
Diamond: Death and his water babes.

Rainbow Changes   12/6/10

Where it is most meant
on the day arrived
prestigious forbearing amidst
the towers of Earth
monumental spaced masses
boarding passageway to
another time and
place when no other
is seen again
there where the blind
trees grow wildly
a force felt amongst
others daring to be

Throes of death
It is painful
To endure
An evening song
Intended for you
The deeply lamented
Dearest but still
Recently departed
Of the temperament
Known to last

Ways   12/9/10

The thyme devoured
Does not lend a rhyme so soured
As to the bric-a-brac
Ways of lying in the sack
With the mighty pack
Up during wild hour.

Once sound,
but the feeling is one
of so high a mountain:
to enjoy all,
feelings coming in
bountifully;
the spirit of livelihood
expressing vivaciously
how to be this kind
of youthful being.

Stronger than imagination holds
limits greater than the
oxen, and riper too than
a newly planted tree,
is courage beyond might,
more ennobling, humbly forsaking
tomorrow's journey,
to meditate and ponder on.

They speak
as it comes to their minds,
laying by the fire,
scorned from the Earth
itself,
away on a journey
which begins when it ends.

Then they said:
another day, another feeling
emitted out of flame,
drawing its power in the
wake of destruction;
to no end does it stop
in mortal sight,
its beastly livelihood.

Fire consumed the flesh
of many souls,
their kin dreadfully
withered from its cast iron
framework,
towering over more than
the land gives way to;
yet another path viewed.

(Distilled water places)
Merry men dancing
a ritual out through the
night,

treading lightly on shifting
space, moving ground and
animal alike towards all
corners.

Spiritual enlightenment braces upon
my being, the past
speaking itself clearly
out loud;
wastrels fear emptiness
of pockets as heathens
do purpose:
a day.

So the ship wrecked
itself on our shores,
people came to see,
enjoy what cargo it had,
excuses such as cleaning
up the beaches—
jolly people they must be,
still.

And drunkards do weep
as the last poison is
seen coming down from
the sky above,
their innards warmed
up and taking a right
beating,
till darkness overwhelms them.

Shredding papier-mâché
gleefully all around the party,

children laugh and smile and
marvel,
imaginations running high
at the wondrous figures
floating down with a
prized package.

No mushroom skies—
cataclysm averted once again.
Stargazers and seers
look ahead at a time
when,
possibility taken into allowance,
abominations will never
be a dream we had.

Soothing,
water can be,
I watch on a clear spring
day the waterfall about
me, reminiscing on past
glories conquered here
while writing in
dribs and drabs.

But it is true
that when horses use
their sense, something
must be about,
whether or not it's just
their way—or fancy—
keen knowledge of circumstance or
insanity.

The sun reveals
this curious episode:
two strangers meet,
a bitter contest against
the shadow realm of ignorance begins.
Both contenders have strength,
courage,
and a profound weakness towards each other.

The simplest of creatures
and elegant,
ladybugs
are a delicacy, even while
observed on the ceiling,
trying to find their way.
Sometimes they pile together on the
windowsill, one next to the other.

The living arts—
movies, theater, a zoo,
getting lost while traveling—
even curious decorative art
on lichen-held
rocks,
all over the world,
bedazzle the touch.

Dead carapaces being
used for shelter,
critters wander about
purposefully
through its one-way
street, searching for life

as the next animal equips
the suit of armor.

Only a little ways
out,
it's all quiet at sea,
as storms move above,
lightning bolts making potshots
that blast gushes of water
upwards towards the gray
heavens.

Endlessly boring tunnels
in his marvelous domain,
the badger knows
underground terrain and,
like a rabbits' enclave,
the job never quite
ends—though he died
today.

Worlds are violent places,
devastating in how they get
around.
With that, even in a
state of flux does it
appear vague to the outsider,
forever remaining the obstinate
ignoramus, saying "I do not know."

Symptoms   12/23/10

Occasionally, you get
people—
so unique are they—
who expose truths
within us.
Darkly flamed, yes,
and deadly too,
as the feelings
grow colder on every
particular morning.

Symptoms strung round,
chords so lightly plucked,
music calling forth
sound waves of joy upon
the finer senses.

Desire

That which we cannot
have,
forced to repress our
feelings,
tearing our hearts out
with spades of blue hue,
beating us down by the
number of times we spent
seeking victory over the
object of hidden affections.

And here a little—
maybe even there—
they notice.
All you can do is
cry inside,
crying for freedoms' sake,
tasting a rare ambrosia
meant for the gods,
producing joy and triumph.

Then the failure
to ever meet
our goal, hoping
that this eternal
misery ends today.
But when it doesn't
do we painfully acknowledge

our status and pitiful
state of being alone.

And slowly do we
see what was clear (now still),
unmoved by
nature's stark reality today,
frozen, as it were,
amidst the echoes of time,
when all but adventure
was seen as idleness.

Conditions speak of words,
feelings ever addressed
round the fireplace,
where a young family
resides, struggling, aye,
but continuing the cycle
of life, keeping alive
the burning spirit.

Hollow sounds the wind;
calmly the thistles go,
their prickliness a bold
attempt in hiding;
trees whereupon the
axe fell, whispers the
winter squirrel on a
cold morning
this day.

Present in a book
laying outside to be read
at a later time,
history speaks fervently
to all who care to hear
and see, as invisible
fingers guide music
through the wild steppes.

The past of people we
remember—even during a
winter storm—
is here now upon us:
a prelude to the opening
of what has been:
so often we find that
then, like now,
is always the same.

I think, and thoughts
appear across my mind.
Is it this way
they lead me,
or will I lose the battle
on some foreign frontier?
My friends promise to never
forget me,
but I do—
I forget them all,
for my thoughts come
in all sizes,
my well-being a priority
only when it is not,
and that is a problem.
Yet in wonderment,
does this make a roving
mind such as mine
last forever?
Or, like all the rest,
be made and spun and
twisted as a new miracle,
an invention as sane as its
maker, yet translating
into mere dust?

A short interlude in
a transient mode from here
to there, back again,

over the mountain twice,
riding a stallion,
so we end here.

Together they go,
dead souls who hate the
past,
remembering what it was
like to feel.

O how hatred is an
all-consuming fire,
eating every last bit
of love away,
turning it into a construct
of demonic proportions.

It's not good to lust
when savory kisses go afoul,
trying your best to
win favors again by
the very people who gave
up on you, who forsook
you, giving up all hope
of ever healing you,
yet stood by, and at
a glance—maybe it went
amiss—did you honor,
and spoke to you,
acknowledging you were
here and well,
amongst ilk bearing
symbols resembling you;

and all you have to do
is ask why did I
ever get such
treatment?

The power of people
is of many sources,
well-defined as they may
be in books,
but to others who heed
not their history,
learn by mistakes if wisdom
of that sort is within,
or go on down the
same damned path
by people
speaking behind their backs,
of bad luck, disrespecting
life, and loathing the world;
and so they give it the
same service.

What a lonely sort to be
stuck as, for today is
a holiday like any other,
one to sing songs of joy on,
even when no one understands
your turn of mind.
Maybe a bend or two from
the straight and narrow
path often taken, and then
maybe by the exotic
that life offers,

but still remaining here,
O you unlearned people,
devouring yourselves
both in and out.

And so march forth!
You pitiful dead-souled
people, you who blaspheme
against life to its utmost
extremes, who traduce and
spite, worshippers of the
Sophist movement, be gone
from our world—
and we mean now!

Gone at last
(that damned fool),
he died well amongst
the drifting meadows,
holding him until his
life faded away.
Yet it continued ever onwards,
searching the forgotten maps
of a spirit
yet to be discovered,
like fungus under a rock,
there it grows.
He searched well until
he saw his way,
ended by dreaming and
never but a thought
left in seeming.

Doom,
in all its seasons,
wandering down the dark
alleyway that is the soul.

It catches and snares
rather nastily with a hooked
ending—all the unsuspecting
people.

Unfinished purposes, randomized
thoughts, to a bitter end
yet to meet, it will and does
make its mark known.

An undreamt medley of thoughts
gone to waste by the wayside:
yet another talent ruined in
someone's presence.

The future may not be told,
but we see possibility and
arrive where we will best
be suited.

Then again, in all events,
closures prevent those actions;
a long time between, memory fades,
we forget the way.

Taking a false step after
many rights, fallen
from our natural state,
a change.

We are graced with the
might and wisdom to do,
this time, today, the time
again, to get out and do.

Esoteric words are against
the flow of truth, we seek
simplicity in order to
create growth of purpose.

Trees must remain as a sign
whispered to us about life in
its excellence, and prevent the
onslaught that is doom.

This seen: damnable
foes in bliss—they stop
to breathe in their ignorance.
Strength in numbers—maybe—
but haven't the mercy
in you to follow broken
paths, uninspired by
life's torment, for the
bane of the living is
uncertainty of the future
after death.

Oddities, randomness, and
plagues upon the
human soul have never
kept us from being who
we want to be.

Truly it is in us, with
a direct and forward
way, to do and be as
we desire, in one fashion
or another.

So when you drink and
offer a toast, do it for
those lost ones who
carry an unlit torch through
their lives.

A damned procession proceeds
against the door of salvation,
unknowingly writing off its soul
with magic dust,
traitors to their people,
selfish in their ways,
not accepting guidance towards
truth or any road that leads
to honesty and goodness.

Yet, they claim they are
charitable, may even donate
money and time to those suffering
more than they, but, in reserved
nature, cast out any care long
ago, forgetting—or nay, not hearing—
lessons on being merciful and
helpful when in power to be so.

Saddened are angels, with misty
eyes and cataractfuls of tears
flowing down from their youthful
faces, innocent of any charge of
guilt, yet understanding those with.

So we try helping—but often failing—
the poor and wretched but unlamented
damned people from their own
self-destruction, seeing
reasons moving without a reason,

but ever there in case
the bell is rung.

Watching the currents
so soothingly calm,
you turn on your back now,
swimming, ripples billowing in
the water, caressing your
ideal form—
and never an unhappy
moment in existence.

On we go, moving in
a natural rhythm,
our bodies underneath
this wide open sea,
following a tone known
so well, lightly feeling
the way, a destination
rediscovered.

Beating time, following
this darkly-lit path,
a cry exceeds my pace.
Wondering at the new shade
of color now entering
all around, you lapse,
wailing in concentrated form.

And I go up to you,
curious of the change,
nudging your nearly inert body;
I look at you,

eyes with shadowy movements
about them, beckoning in that
moment, and say:
I am here with you.

Soft touches in your
voice—an invitation to dance
in the primitive;
a shared but secret
bath together,
forbidden lusts untamed,
manifesting themselves this
night, showing our true
selves, what and who
we are.

(The next morning,
after the wild night)
What was it? We called
each other names, fanciful and
free from the weight of
the world, but with meaning.
A wonderful time spent.
My best friend called,
worried, asking why
I missed our nightly
phone call.

How can one wrapped
in desire answer so common
a request? I confessed,
and was lessened by one
amongst friends. Time
and mercy may see to my

forgiveness, but I feel
no shame in my actions
towards my kind, being
embalmed only with love.

Humble and weak,
bound by class,
wicked to the last,
nonstop fun—
this is the way
we get things done
on a misty day,
a day of metaphor
and fakeries,
liars and bakeries;
corrupted art smells
alongside broken down wishing wells;
desolate walkways in bad repair,
leading one to absolutely nowhere.
Rained-on orphans are all around,
having come in from the backside of town.

When in doubt
we look for a way out,
seeing only a branch falling
that clubs us hard, lulling
us to a fitful sleep
that promises to be oh-so-very deep.

I hope you were alright
while lying together,
feeling each other over,
lovers in a mood swing,
emotions running high,
loving you all the time,
never letting go.

We cuddle up to one another,
embracing, kissing, touching,
feeling
every last bit,
entangled, not letting go,
fearing we might escape each other—
but loving always.

Speak the words so
sweetly until this
part of my hidden
heart is revealed:
missing you since the Earth began,
kissing you with Prometheus' fire,
seeing you as my Guinevere,
being there beside me.

To fated feelings, bold
under a spell we hold
from times of solitude,
we share this.

To those we espied,
a fly so nimble—
Oh! It's the size of a thimble!
These nonsense scribblings lied.

To your darkly-humored ways,
all the world as one
is under my gaze: the setting sun,
blinding us as we pass the days.

And to your not-so-delightful
but happy pleasure—spent,
I think, in leisure; decorative boxes
made to fit your touch.

That which sees, prepare:
flying kites that swear,
all in a whirl, even in
ones personal nightmare.

Wells of temperate storms rely
on and for the sake of
a gray-chiseled sky.
The moon was up during
a rocky day; obsidian
structures collapsed, revealing
former strengths and weaknesses;
marbled attired and
chaste-felt-but-opaque
jet hands,
those and a ruby feel fill
all sound, leaving only the
direst of needs to remain.

To say, and more, to do,
when there was nothing,
leaving the leaves on rivers
overflowing into a mind not
ripe with torture; heady
notions of tranquility vanish
below the lodge facing an
infinite cliff, with wandering
hills surrounded in
overabundant beauty,
yet all of this
is missing from the evil
landscape, bereft of soul
and an essence stolen during
the endless age of existence,

where it is found to be lost
without a reason; and when
that random event occurs,
yes, we know there is a
purpose to the longings of the
lamented but truly damned
individuals both in life and
in death, condemning them forever.

A spirit that walks through time
and does not falter—
yet with a cruel face
and a daring mind
may enter the holy place
which no mortal being
has denied from existing.
O spirit, what a subtly reluctant
way you have when dealing
with lust—
or is this a shade of shyness
in your paling form?
The bile tracked upon a fallen
pedestal seeks an heir,
and coming from a
damned source,
will most certainly have you.

Not my day, you say?
Yet feeling the zest
of a youthful spirit
and a calling that says:
I am alive. Hear me and
know this: everyday is my day,
whether I feel good on it
or am stricken with an illness
of another kind. What kind?
Pray thee tell. The wind withers
a thousand times before reaping
the sands of faith,
and still have I yet
to reveal a nature dreamt
of in the visions that call me
here in this diurnal realm,
its scope fathomable only to those
who believe that when fantasies
become reality,
dreams become the
shadows we feel but once,
and then they're gone.

Temple   4/29/13

At the atrium complex
where stars unite in the
heavens' glory
sits a seeker
who finds themselves
alone on a cold mountain top,
pondering the meaning to being.
"This way," they say—
but why not the other?
The seeker does not
know the answer,
yet from a preternatural gift
of thought,
may perforce have the energy
to lift their eyes above
and know that anything great
in the world of existence
is always beyond the
simple reaches of what
we can perceive;
and so life takes place.

The air,
delightful and cheap:
it one day breathed,
and while we depended
on its resuscitative powers,
opted to rest,
so coming to a speedy
end, this writing.

Truth   6/9/13

Moments of quietude end;
brittle rocks shatter,
and another disaster
leaves mention on my
Sunday table.

While away,
time speaks to me;
laughter in words
melt all faded fears
from realizing myself
out of ruptured solitude.

Saints' grass I tread,
arriving in peace,
watching two colors
become one . . .
and it was quiet.

Rampant winds conquered
the bastard title of
a forgotten castle,
casting its last stone
down.

And when sorrow met
vengeance, a meeting
was held, trust gained in an
odd way, but both
very much present in the world.

While the sheep looked
up, a farmer stole
them. That is all
reported from yesteryear's
Green Pastures magazine.

Xenophobic frogs at
a jester's conclave
found their mutual
ties bounded by water
drawn from a well.

The king held a
false assembly of
badgers and squirrels,
reassuring his mad reign
over the animal world.

The swift seasons' calming
effects soothe the
dead bodies of
lawyers, doctors, politicians,
and insurance salesmen,
priming them for
collectability.

Travels from a
highlander's perspective
go unseen, yet mean
nothing but the
thorns found on a
holly bush, signifying warning
of what is said.

Bunnies times a
billion along the
wayside; what that
means, and what
my psychologist interprets
it as are of two
different worlds.

Faded tavern signs
once used on a
prestigious movie set;
now the abyss
begins, an unlovely
sight, and killable
as well.

Mink mugs is where
our products end,

but just below us
you may find frosted
tails of indescribable
beasts, but with claims
of validity made.

Diseases made from
standing in motion too
long are designed
around concrete bases
not weighed down by
issuances of
questionable merit.

Flatter heads on
a rolling block;
quaint, the motif
resounding like that
of a desiccated
tune played backwards
on board a sinking ship.

But the humans who
live won't bring relief,
so those who tempt
are favored by
mischievously turned creatures,
experimenting with fabled
but torched words.

Of soiled texture is
a ripe and fattened
balloon ready to burst,
just as a man

steps in and offers
to fix what ails
the flawed framework.

Only two made it,
yet from the
darker imagination did
bedlam take place,
and we find ourselves
within a tapered
structure.

Living past succeeding
movements,
an aria collapsed,
producing waves of
cheering, and making
the whole establishment
know what the audience
really wanted to see.

Impish stares among
shoppers at windows,
the glass deciding to give
in and break.
When this happened,
happiness and merriment
amused idle gods
from their waking dreams.

Moving along with restricting
thoughts,
the Apple girl went
on her lonely way,

singing out what
could not be held in;
the Apple family found
their cold seedling.

(Separating was never easy,
but cousins do it too)
The fissure began
by swallowing old hearts,
then grew a taste
for newborns—
fair indeed for
neutral nature—
but wasn't happy,
so the ground sank
in and was lost,
as were all lives;
but with an interesting
artistry all about how
it came about,
the account from which
this is based cannot
be said to be original.

Creation was with the
world, but then it lapsed
into another form, a
differing state from
how things this way
normally turn out.
Eventually it got the
task right, and found
things that moved more

than once after settling
down in a single spot.

As progress continued,
many crashes and mistakes
jokingly occurred (if you
could see this, you would
smile too), but about
the time another
accident was about to
happen, the day
rested and forgot
itself all over,
leaving only bleak
memories of what
was there before
the end.

Having breath silently
crossing its back,
a new world awakes,
one of plenitude
and diversity.

As like is to like,
so must different
worlds be different.

The greatest sin upon the land,
to every lamb, woman, and man,
a calling of an unbearable loss
to speak against the rosy toss
of an inflated coin, a false kind of
merriment, but bearing a lad's stable and gloved
hand, which on beautiful land was loved;
and off we go on another round of Poe.

Over soft, moldy hills
an effort was raised with
nothing but smooth, crested
oaken barrels; where perfection
exists, the builder hurries
the creaking along, careful
to measure another board
with beautiful variety.
And where do the rabbits
rest now? Over by that
new log cabin where a
tinker stores his old
body.

Days are far too long
waiting to die, but a slow
movement played by
saccharin-infused strings (with a
touch of algae) dust away
any regrets I
shared with others.
A pixelated existence, the
fake leaf draws no more
attention when deleted.

On the edge of oblivion,
a fairy staring wildly learns
new games, making for a fresher,
more feral fairy; and still

during the night, it is
welcomed back to the enclave
with more partying and
gestures than a purple heron's
spouse could endure.

Over the rainbow bridge,
fire-speckled matter permeates
throughout the wooden exterior,
finally seeing it collapse
without fanfare.

Diurnal thinking produces dust spattered
caringly over me,
reflecting off my lambent eyes;
my shredded mind, however,
catapults itself from
within a fellow spectator.

And who will this haunted
spirit's next choice be?
Will it make someone cry,
or taint a letter sent off to
a hate-filled audience?
Or will it torture itself
into believing that the
help it offers really does
do that? But somehow it misses,
and causes agony and grief.

So the world began with a bang;
and so it will end with
 a whimper.

Sadness is the feeling to
have when at a tombstone,
sitting in the ponderer's
position, breathing a skunk's
relief through flamed nostrils.

Happy they are gone so
their Lord and Father
may judge them eternally;
happy am I, feeling the
granite's texture, putting me
in a stony mood;
happier still are they who
were given what wasn't
theirs, so that they may
never meet their dearly departed
on the other side.

Warmth, the feeling of a
saint all day by their friends'
side—the whole world is their
friend—by a roadside steeple
and chapel, where sinners
are blessed and condemned
and forgotten.

Light with showy flower
pistils are a haven to those
who know how to use them;
and the remembered brethren

who shake our heads until
we are crazy; they too
we solemnly forgave yesterday.

Those without a feather to
spare shall be thought of
thrice; once seriously, once
in a joking rhyme, and a
third to place permanently
somewhere.

Somewhere a white lily pad is
floating to a chasm of rather
tedious depths, but while it
flows over it, a day that
began with lament and sorrow
shall see a sign that
tells those dreary people:
alright, time to do some
hiking and talking to yourself more!

Waning birds are caught in an
updraft; before long the
soaring animals hit an old
biplane and meet terra firma
quite permanently.

When all of this was over,
I sat myself down by a bench
and read about how long
dawn redwood's have been
around me.

What to Expect on a Saturday Afternoon on Land   8/17/13

Signaling fire, a hurricane
season started off a hazy
pattern that followed my
neighbor wherever he went.

That day he set fire to
a yellowjacket's nest using
some old gasoline can,
then having it burst into a
blaze which destroyed his
barn—that was rather
memorable; and then when I
fell off a tiny rock by
the local brook, it hit
my funny bone, and must've
cracked it, for the crazy
laughter I created made even
the squirrels laugh.

The pages I had drawn from
faded memories escaped me
in that the ink went dry
on spots that meant much
to me.

Along lost forest paths
there exists a battered
statue of a demon. Created out
of a night's spiteful charm,
it had also been overwhelmed

by a claw hammer's striking
it which thereby shattered
the left side's eye, and
left instead a fierce,
if broken stare which promised
anyone who crossed it a possible
mouthful of food—if it were, indeed,
alive.

Remembering the destruction of the
town's Catholic Church made
the rabbi smile a gleeful
little naughty joy only he
would divulge to the man who
replaced him.

Xenophobic ears were cut
off by righteous knights who
fervently believed they were
merely helping the victims
change their beliefs—and
with the added benefit of
losing weight.

Over by a footpath, a snake
wandered too far and fell
into an ancient well
dug some seven thousand years ago
and signed "A&J."

The soft dry leaves
rest on moss-covered timber,
another day burning an etched press
of moonlit dawns.

Whispering gently, redwood branches
awaken the pollinating air,
reaching all the way down to a grassy knoll
with a secret entrance.

Again as time strains a
last candle towards the sky,
forgotten lamentations summon
wispy breathing for the day.

Stilled temples within
a hollow body form the
setting for a ritual to bring it
down to the hallowed ground.

Sudden but vivacious movements
behind swollen hills; and
a bee died this day
from a giant hand.

Crawling along a soggy
path, a drowned leaf
prays to let its saturation
reveal life's meaning.

Smoky-but-certain-eyes
disappear into a
wilderness that knows where
it was.

Clarity comes from within,
as does an angel believing
in what that forest fire
did last year.

Singed apricots, coupled with
ashen-laden bread crumbs fulfill
the previous stanza's destructive
commitments.

Buttoning up for church,
the priest wanders if what
he's about to tell the
victims is truly relevant.

Beneath a glimmering fountain,
darkness dispels any knowledge
of happy moments as the
day forgot what light is.

Gathering strength is what
this day is about,
walking along a rather
fortunately-found creek,
one I never knew of before.
Helping myself to the cool breeze,
I traveled amongst the
boulder-strewn country as
if surveying my land (which
it was, for that moment,
as no one else was
here to claim it).

Keen of vision and might,
assisted with grace and
blessed in perseverance,
I was beckoned to continue
what turned out to be a
slightly more than usual
day for me.

But it really was fairly
typical, and only as I
approached the great old
beast did I notice the
store benches set forever
in their place, as if it
was some pagan place of
worship I was seeing.

The tree stood out from
the rest because it stood
apart, and so was alone in
a family of plenty, though in
its many years, the ancient
white oak had begotten
most of the woods around it.
One year a powerful
storm came to the secluded
spot, cast out a thunderbolt
from its weaponry, and oh! There
goes the monster's left
upper arm—or branch, really—
never to be seen attached again.

It is now that I see
this former beauty queen
as an aged relic, not doing
terribly well, yet maintaining
an aura of grace.
Plenty of visitors have passed
her, always noticing that her
primordial powers have been
extinguished.

In spirit, the essence
portrayed on a few lives
permits itself to recognizing
that a portrait of relish
isn't the stable of society.

When angled in to further depths,
commonly placed people do the
stupidly bold moves that
make names for yet more
six-day wonders.

Having a mere whimsy of a
notion of what was said
formerly, but still going on in
rambling nonsense, I hear
what three hundred and sixty is.

If in degrees, says the
listener, then make it
better than who came
before you, for, you well
know, that powers only
last during the times they
are spelled out.

Situational depressions set
back the economy, while writing
about it does not. How then
can astute teachers fail

to teach their patients
this primal fact?

Failing with glamour,
the pixie king oversaw
what his senatorial council
wrote, and knew it to
be more daily rubbish
for him to digest and
digress on; until later he
decided to destroy it, then it
was a good day.

Having used up privileges
for nine years, all the
peoples' claims were thrown
down into a negating bucket,
to be used in later publications
at the sole insanity of
the editor.

Wildebeests slain in battle were
given high decorative awards
for being in such stately
conditions as the mortician
appraised them, drooling all the while.
He only wished for an encore,
and that would more than
delight his otherwise ideal day.

To end, in wit, is to die,
be dead, go on to the next world,
and solemnly swear your eternal
sins in a mute witness's repose.

With all but the most hateful
moments seen in an invisible life,
the destroyer walked along an
ancient road, whose surface had seen
much battling along its shapely
contours, searching for another
life to desecrate, all
to make itself alive again.

Through the empty metal door,
the knocking persists,
vibrating along blank corners
of foreboding.
While this happens,
a massive and grotesque *thing* out of
a story reveals itself, a spawn
of warped circumstances,
and the glowing lights can
only mean that we have reached
our utmost destination.
So it is with glee that I leap
from this spacecraft and
explore the sunken depths
of a new world.

When is the right light
seen on those perfectly
falling days? Then when
we say goodbye and
mean it, there is a little
sacred dance we play
with again.

Having settled, no more
"when" to life: throw them
all out, break the glass mirror,
smash whatever needs smashing,
quell people's voices,
sing gaily while doing it,
and never forget that
"when" is also a time.

When, on the day it
happens, and some are
happy, there occurs this
state, and such is that
happenstance where a withered
baseball knots itself, hidden
away, and found by some lost
wanderer driven by a thirst
for knowledge.
Never was it justified clearly,
but happily we will not know
the ending, just that it happens
to some people.

Notes

Notes

The poems written on 8/17/13 and 8/29/13, being "Mere Trivialities," " ''Life's Little Everythings''," "What to Expect on a Saturday Afternoon on Land," "Just Another Day," "Gathering Along a Stream in Autumn," and "Happy Lines Written," were all written on the same wooden bench in The Village of Arden. Every other poem was written at home. This likely affected the way they turned out, and so I thought to mention it as they were produced under different circumstances (they were both warm and sunny days, after all).

ABOUT THE AUTHOR

Daniel Robert Lewis was born in Wilmington, Delaware, in 1986, and has published many other books, which include poetry, short fiction, humor, essays, and philosophy. He has every intention of adding more genres to his repertoire in the near future.

Made in the USA
Middletown, DE
31 May 2024

54865752R00076